DIGGING UP THE PAST

KING TUT'S TOMB

BY TRUDY BECKER

WWW.APEXEDITIONS.COM

Copyright © 2026 by Apex Editions, Mendota Heights, MN 55120. All rights reserved. No part of this book may be reproduced or utilized in any form or by any means without written permission from the publisher.

Apex is distributed by North Star Editions:
sales@northstareditions.com | 888-417-0195

Produced for Apex by Red Line Editorial.

Photographs ©: Uwe Anspach/picture-alliance/dpa/AP Images, cover; Library of Congress, 4–5; Hulton Archive/Getty Images, 6–7; Shutterstock Images, 1, 8–9, 10–11, 14, 16–17, 21, 26, 27, 29; iStockphoto, 12–13; Art Images/Culture Club/Hulton Fine Art Collection/Getty Images, 18; Art Media/Print Collector/Hulton Archive/Getty Images, 19; John Keates/Alamy, 20; Bettmann/Getty Images, 22–23, 24; Saedi Press/AP Images, 25

Library of Congress Control Number: 2025930915

ISBN
979-8-89250-532-1 (hardcover)
979-8-89250-568-0 (paperback)
979-8-89250-638-0 (ebook pdf)
979-8-89250-604-5 (hosted ebook)

Printed in the United States of America
Mankato, MN
082025

NOTE TO PARENTS AND EDUCATORS
Apex books are designed to build literacy skills in striving readers. Exciting, high-interest content attracts and holds readers' attention. The text is carefully leveled to allow students to achieve success quickly. Additional features, such as bolded glossary words for difficult terms, help build comprehension.

CHAPTER 1
SECRETS IN THE SAND 4

CHAPTER 2
KING TUT 10

CHAPTER 3
TOMB TREASURES 16

CHAPTER 4
LEARNING FROM THE TOMB 22

COMPREHENSION QUESTIONS • 28
GLOSSARY • 30
TO LEARN MORE • 31
ABOUT THE AUTHOR • 31
INDEX • 32

CHAPTER 1

SECRETS IN THE SAND

It is a warm day in 1922. A team of **archaeologists** works under the Egyptian sun. The team searches for King Tutankhamun's **tomb**.

Archaeologist Howard Carter led the search for King Tut's tomb.

The tombs of Egypt's rulers were often buried so thieves couldn't find them.

The team hauls rocks. The workers move hot sand. Suddenly, they uncover a shape. It looks like the top of a staircase.

FAST FACT
King Tut's tomb was buried under 150,000 tons (136,000 metric tons) of rock.

After a few weeks of digging, the site is ready to enter. One archaeologist steps down. He lights a candle and looks around. Gold and jewels glitter in the dim light.

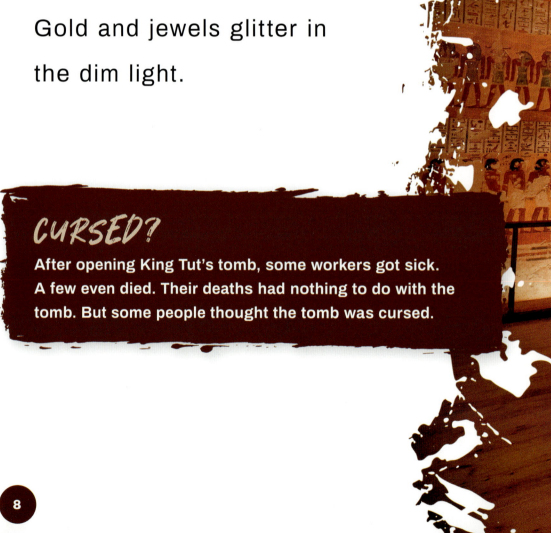

CURSED?

After opening King Tut's tomb, some workers got sick. A few even died. Their deaths had nothing to do with the tomb. But some people thought the tomb was cursed.

King Tut's tomb had several rooms. Archaeologists spent eight years uncovering all of them.

CHAPTER 2

KING TUT

Tutankhamun was an Egyptian ruler. He became pharaoh in 1333 BCE. He was just nine years old. Tut ruled for about 10 years. Then he died.

Many pharaohs had large statues of themselves to show their power.

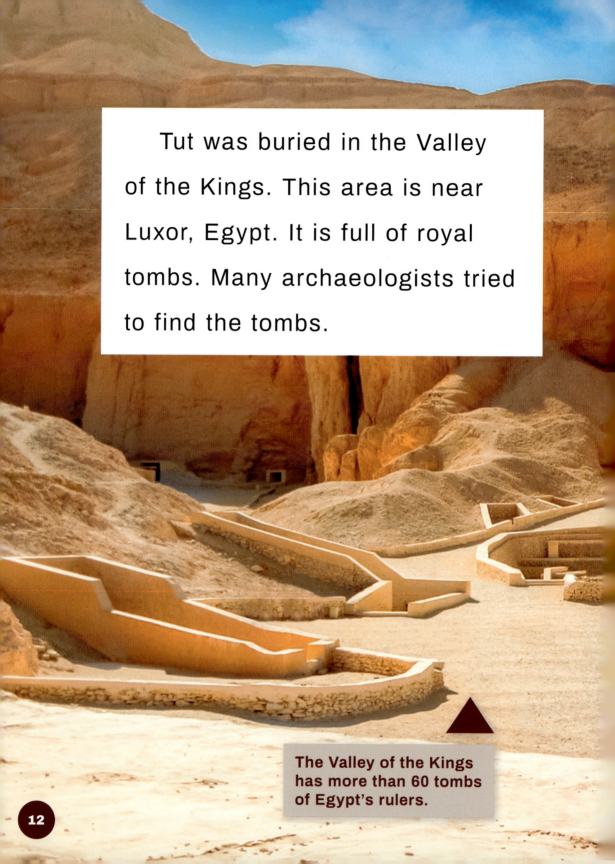

Tut was buried in the Valley of the Kings. This area is near Luxor, Egypt. It is full of royal tombs. Many archaeologists tried to find the tombs.

The Valley of the Kings has more than 60 tombs of Egypt's rulers.

FAST FACT

People knew about King Tut from **ancient** writings. But for 3,000 years, they didn't know where his tomb was.

Pharaohs were buried with lots of treasure. Thieves often tried to steal it. But few robbers found King Tut's tomb. So, it still contained many items.

STOLEN TREASURE

Other pharaohs had bigger tombs than Tut. They were buried with more treasure, too. However, thieves looted the tombs. When archaeologists found them, they were mostly empty.

◀ King Tut's tomb is the most complete Egyptian tomb ever found.

CHAPTER 3

TOMB TREASURES

Tut's tomb had four main rooms. One room held a **casket** with his body. Other rooms were filled with treasure.

16

King Tut was buried with a gold face mask.

Tut's tomb contained several weapons. One was a dagger made from gold and crystal.

Archaeologists found about 5,000 items in Tut's tomb. The tomb had valuable items such as gold and jewelry. It also had everyday things such as toys, clothing, and furniture.

FAST FACT
Tut's tomb included a board game called senet.

King Tut had four sets of senet. Some experts think it was his favorite game.

Tut was buried with 100 pairs of sandals. One pair was made with gold.

Ancient Egyptians believed in an **afterlife**. So, they buried items in tombs for pharaohs to use. They also made pharaohs' bodies into mummies.

MAKING MUMMIES

Ancient Egyptians made mummies to **preserve** bodies. First, they removed the body's **organs**. Next, they dried the body. Then they wrapped it in strips of cloth.

The process of making a mummy took about 70 days.

CHAPTER 4

LEARNING FROM THE TOMB

Researchers studied Tut's tomb carefully. They took many pictures. And they wrote detailed notes. Researchers also brought many items to labs and museums.

Tut's items broke easily. So, researchers had to move them carefully.

Researchers found more than 140 items in Tut's wrappings. Many were made of gold.

In labs, people did more research. They studied King Tut's body. They took apart the mummy and casket. They learned about how ancient Egyptians buried people.

Tut's Body

Researchers have taken many scans of Tut's body. They found that he may have died from an illness. Also, his left foot was hurt. He may have needed a cane to walk.

In 2005, researchers scanned Tut's body. They could see inside the mummy without damaging it.

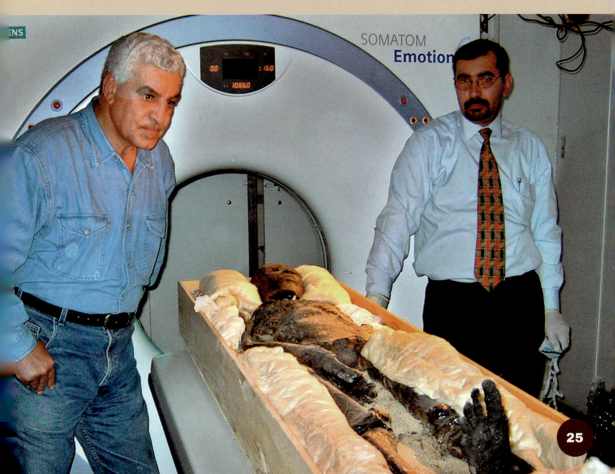

Paintings cover the walls in King Tut's tomb. They show events from his life.

Researchers also studied the tomb's art and items. They learned many things about life in ancient Egypt. The tomb remains a famous and important find.

FAST FACT Many items from Tut's tomb are displayed in museums.

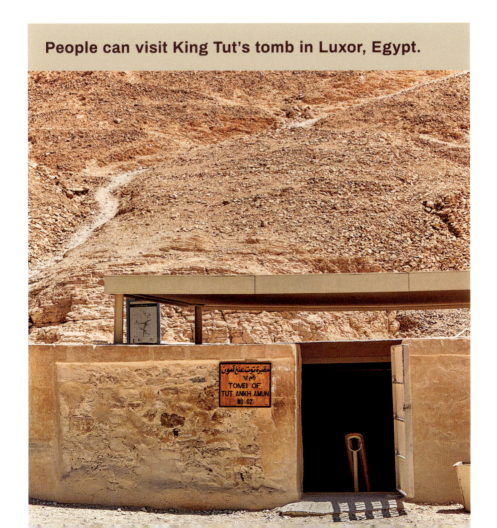

People can visit King Tut's tomb in Luxor, Egypt.

27

COMPREHENSION QUESTIONS

Write your answers on a separate piece of paper.

1. Explain the main ideas of Chapter 2.

2. Would you like to be an archaeologist? Why or why not?

3. How many items were in King Tut's tomb?

    A. 1,333
    B. about 5,000
    C. more than 150,000

4. Why did ancient Egyptians include everyday items in pharaohs' tombs?

    A. They thought the pharaohs would need those items in the afterlife.
    B. The pharaohs went into their tombs before they died.
    C. The pharaohs were not rich enough to have treasure.

5. What does **hauls** mean in this book?

*The team **hauls** rocks. The workers move hot sand. Suddenly, they uncover a shape.*

- **A.** moves something
- **B.** eats something
- **C.** writes on something

6. What does **valuable** mean in this book?

*The tomb had **valuable** items such as gold and jewelry.*

- **A.** not very expensive
- **B.** worth lots of money
- **C.** made out of paper

Answer key on page 32.

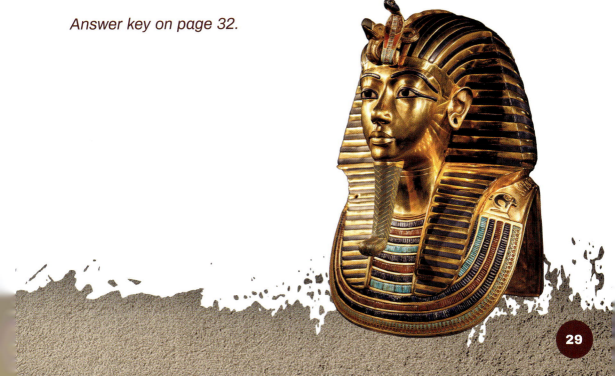

GLOSSARY

afterlife
A place some people believe spirits go after death.

ancient
Very old or from long ago.

archaeologists
People who study long-ago times, often by digging up things from the past.

casket
A box in which a dead person is buried.

organs
Parts of the body that do certain jobs. Organs include the heart, lungs, and kidneys.

preserve
To protect something so that it does not change.

tomb
A place where a dead person is buried.

BOOKS

Gieseke, Tyler. *Egyptian Gods and Goddesses*. Abdo Publishing, 2022.

Murray, Julie. *King Tut's Tomb*. Abdo Publishing, 2022.

Oachs, Emily Rose. *King Tut's Tomb*. Bellwether Media, 2020.

ONLINE RESOURCES

Visit **www.apexeditions.com** to find links and resources related to this title.

ABOUT THE AUTHOR

Trudy Becker lives in Minneapolis, Minnesota. She likes exploring new places and loves anything involving books.

INDEX

A
afterlife, 20
archaeologists, 4, 7–8, 12, 15, 18
art, 26

C
casket, 16, 24

G
gold, 8, 18

L
Luxor, Egypt, 12

M
mummies, 20–21, 24
museums, 22, 27

P
pharaohs, 10, 15, 20

S
senet, 19

T
thieves, 15
treasure, 15, 16

V
Valley of the Kings, 12

ANSWER KEY:
1. Answers will vary; 2. Answers will vary; 3. B; 4. A; 5. A; 6. B